2

DESIGNER'S GUIDE TO JAPANESE
PATTERNS

JEANNE ALLEN

Original book concept
by Takashi Katano

CHRONICLE BOOKS ■ SAN FRANCISCO

■ CONTENTS

**First published in the United States 1988 by
Chronicle Books**

English text copyright © 1988 by Chronicle Books.

Copyright © 1987 by Kawade Shobo Shinsha Publishers. All rights reserved. No part of this book may
be reproduced in any form without written permis-
sion from Chronicle Books.

Printed in Japan.

Edo Mon-yo Jiten by Takashi Katano was first
published in Japan by Kawade Shobo Shinsha
Publishers.

Library of Congress Cataloging in Publication Data

Allen, Jeanne, 1945–
    Designer's guide to Japanese patterns. 2.

    Based on: Edo mon'yō jiten / Katano Takashi.
    1. Decoration and ornament—Japan—Themes,
motives.
    I. Katano, Takashi, 1934–   Edo mon'yō jiten.
    II. Title.
    NK1484.A1A45   1988   745.4′4952   88-21679
    ISBN 0-87701-549-X
    ISBN 0-87701-543-0 (pbk.)

Edited by Terry Ryan
Cover design by Karen Pike
Translation by Nobata Mitsui
Typesetting by TBH Typecast

Distributed in Canada by Raincoast Books,
112 East Third Avenue, Vancouver, B.C., V5T 1C8

10   9   8   7   6   5   4   3   2   1

Chronicle Books
275 Fifth Street
San Francisco, California
94103

■ INTRODUCTION

Designer's Guide to Japanese Patterns 2 is a compilation of patterns from Japan's artistically explosive Edo period (1603–1868), described by one historian as "A boisterous, riotous time . . . when everyone is wearing gay and costly brocades, and even servants spend all they have for kimono."

Prior to the Edo period, Japan had spent centuries under the rigid rule of nobility and samurai who kept the country embroiled in internal and external wars, leaving little time for cultural development and personal opportunity for the middle classes. When the Tokugawa shogunate came to power in 1603, however, Japan experienced its first period of sustained peace in the country's long history.

After assuming control, the Tokugawas respectfully yet quickly moved the seat of power from the festering imperial court in Kyoto to a simple camp in a bleak marshland known as Edo (modern-day Tokyo), where Japan was to build a new society. Attracted by new possibilities and greater personal freedoms, people from every class soon flocked to this makeshift city.

Under the Tokugawas, the class distinctions that had dictated Japanese life for so long became at first blurred and then totally redefined. The enforced peace imposed by the shogunate replaced war as daily fare, and the samurai, previously at the top of the social order, became anachronisms, socially and otherwise. The samurai had mixed success in finding new outlets for their talents. Many contributed to the development of an efficient administrative and legal system; some helped advance scholarship and the arts; others, however, were lost souls who couldn't adapt to the new order and watched their wealth, as well as their status, drift away. Many of these developed a well-deserved reputation for bullying and chronic drunkenness, an understandable condition considering the Tokugawas' failure to retrain these bred-in-the-bone warriors for a life of peace.

While the samurai reeled, the merchants and artisans profited handsomely by the new social stability. After satisfying their basic needs, Edo merchants and their families became intoxicated with their newly acquired economic power and greedily indulged their appetites for the luxuries of theater, gambling, and finery. They made idols of their favorite Kabuki actors and superstars of their kimono designers. The introduction of woodblock printing stimulated artists to chronicle this colorful and flamboyant society in depth. Exotic *ukiyo-e* (floating world) prints give a glimpse into the intimacies of geisha life and Kabuki's most dramatic moments.

Fashion and personal adornment—a passion throughout Japanese history—is always indicative of the moment. In Edo, for the first time, style was set by a class other than the court or the samurai. The merchants craved the sumptuous kimono silks and elegant brocaded *obi* that had always been beyond their reach. Their patronage, in turn, richly rewarded the artisans for their creativity and originality and created opportunities for major advances in weaving, dyeing, and stenciling.

Isolated from foreign influences (the shogunate had banned all outside contact), Japanese artists turned their vision inward to examine their Heian heritage and reinterpret these elegant traditional designs with a freshness and spirit characteristic of the Edo mind. The legendary kimono designs inspired by the work of the Kanō and Rimpa artists were a pure Japanese expression free of Chinese influence. Poetic images of maple leaves, cherry blossoms, falling snow, spreading fans, and other themes thought of as "typically Japanese" were just part of the Edo artist's repertory. Generic images from everyday life were also immensely popular. Cart wheels, cooking pots, and woven patterns borrowed from bamboo ceilings are a few of the frankly mundane themes adapted by unrestrained Edo artists to decorate the kimono of their patrons. Eventually, these genre patterns were combined with poetic images that had once been the exclusive property of the aristocracy. By the Genroku era (mid-Edo period), patterns combining such unlikely bedfellows as irises and carpenters' tools began to appear. Riddle patterns that identified the wearer's family, occupation, or thoughts on a particular subject were also typical Edo products—such designs were especially popular among Kabuki actors, their families, and adoring fans.

The citizens of Edo spent much of their leisure time strolling in the parks showing off the latest finery and admiring the chic ensembles of others. These fashion shows were meticulously recorded in woodblock prints, which served as a sort of *Women's Wear Daily* of the time. Cheap and plentiful, the prints were quickly distributed throughout the country to non-Edoites who were eager to learn the news from Japan's style capital. These prints show that the secret of Edo *iki* (chic) did not lie in the expense of the design, but in the simplicity that was also exceptionally stylish.

This simplicity came in handy when the shogunate began to pass sumptuary laws designed to curb the excessive spending of the merchants. Silk, vivid color, and elaborate embroidery were forbidden in kimono and *obi*. Artists were restricted to two colors in woodblock prints. The merchants complied at least outwardly with the edicts and replaced silks with modest cotton stripes in blues and browns. As often as not, though, these externally simple kimono were lined with brightly colored silks that could still be appreciated and admired by those who mattered in the right circles. After a time, the sumptuary laws were relaxed, and the merchants and their families quickly took up where they left off in flashy, flamboyant fashion.

At the end of the Edo period, Japan opened its ports to Western influence, style, and taste to end its self-imposed isolation and the brief, creative vision that represented Edo. Many Japanese people feel that from that time to this—an era sometimes referred to as a second Edo period—nothing original has come from Japanese artists.

About This Book

This collection of 141 designs and patterns belonging exclusively to the Edo period explores and examines the range of artistic moods existing in Japan hundreds of years ago. The designs make up a graphic language that expresses the energy and originality that typified Edo life. Unlike abstract art that is removed from the reality of everyday living, these designs are the intensely personal expressions of ordinary people and, three hundred years later, are still an integral part of Japanese daily life—living legacies of the Edoites' unique vision.

Top
The popular patterns of the Edo period can still be seen in the *ukiyo-e* woodblock prints of the time. This illustration, for instance, shows the waterfall stripe in example 102.

Bottom
Some patterns were used to decorate containers and personal implements. Here, a lacquer lunch box is decorated in gold with a pattern of summer foliage.

1 ■ Waves and Plover

2 ■ **Flowering Plants and Bird**

3 ■ **Moon and Waves**

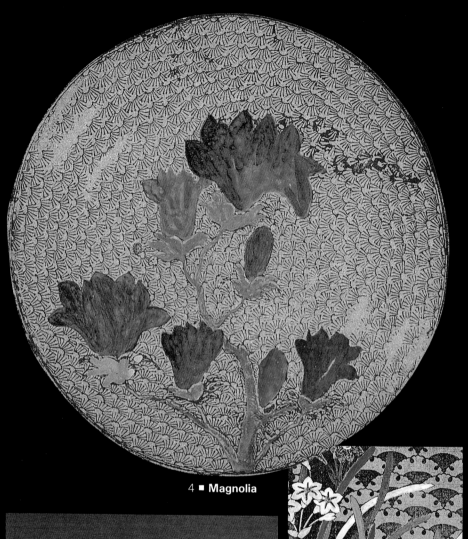

4 ■ Magnolia

5 ■ Boat

6 ■ Snowflakes and Narcissus

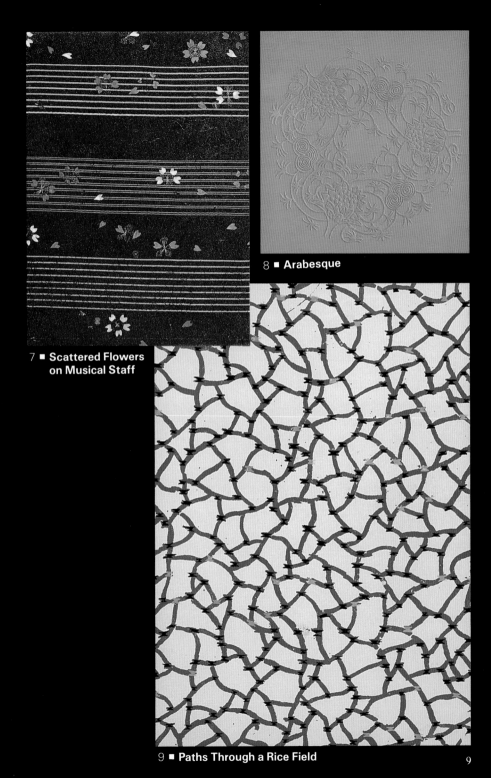

7 ■ Scattered Flowers
on Musical Staff

8 ■ Arabesque

9 ■ Paths Through a Rice Field

10 ■ **Turf in the Snow**   11 ■ **Cherry Blossoms**

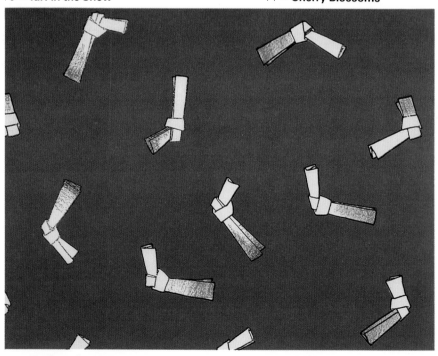

12 ■ **Love Letters**

13 ▪ **Japanese Apricot Blossoms**

14 ■ *Ebōsho* (Decorated Papers from Kyoto)

15 ■ *Ebōsho* (Decorated Papers from Kyoto)

16

16 ■ Autumn Grasses

The designs that we think of as "typically Japanese" were developed during the Edo period—initially by Kanō Tanyu and his followers. Still the standard for refined taste today, the art of Kanō was free of Chinese influence and purged of the flamboyancy that typified the Momoyama period (1576–1603). Subject matter, like the autumn grasses and chrysanthemums in this design, was taken from nature. Such vignettes of visual poetry were skillfully interpreted on silk through elaborate dyeing processes and embroidery.

17 ■ *Ashigawa* **(River Reeds)**
This *komon* (miniature pattern) was borrowed by Edo designers from the Kamakura period (1185–1338). Originally used to decorate battle armor, these small motifs were put on leather by a smoking technique called *kusube*.

18 ■ **Reeds on the Water**
The Edo artist designed patterns that were the visual poetry of their time. In this design, where sunlight seems to reflect off the surface, the verticals represent reeds, the arched shapes represent water grasses, and the short horizontal lines represent water.

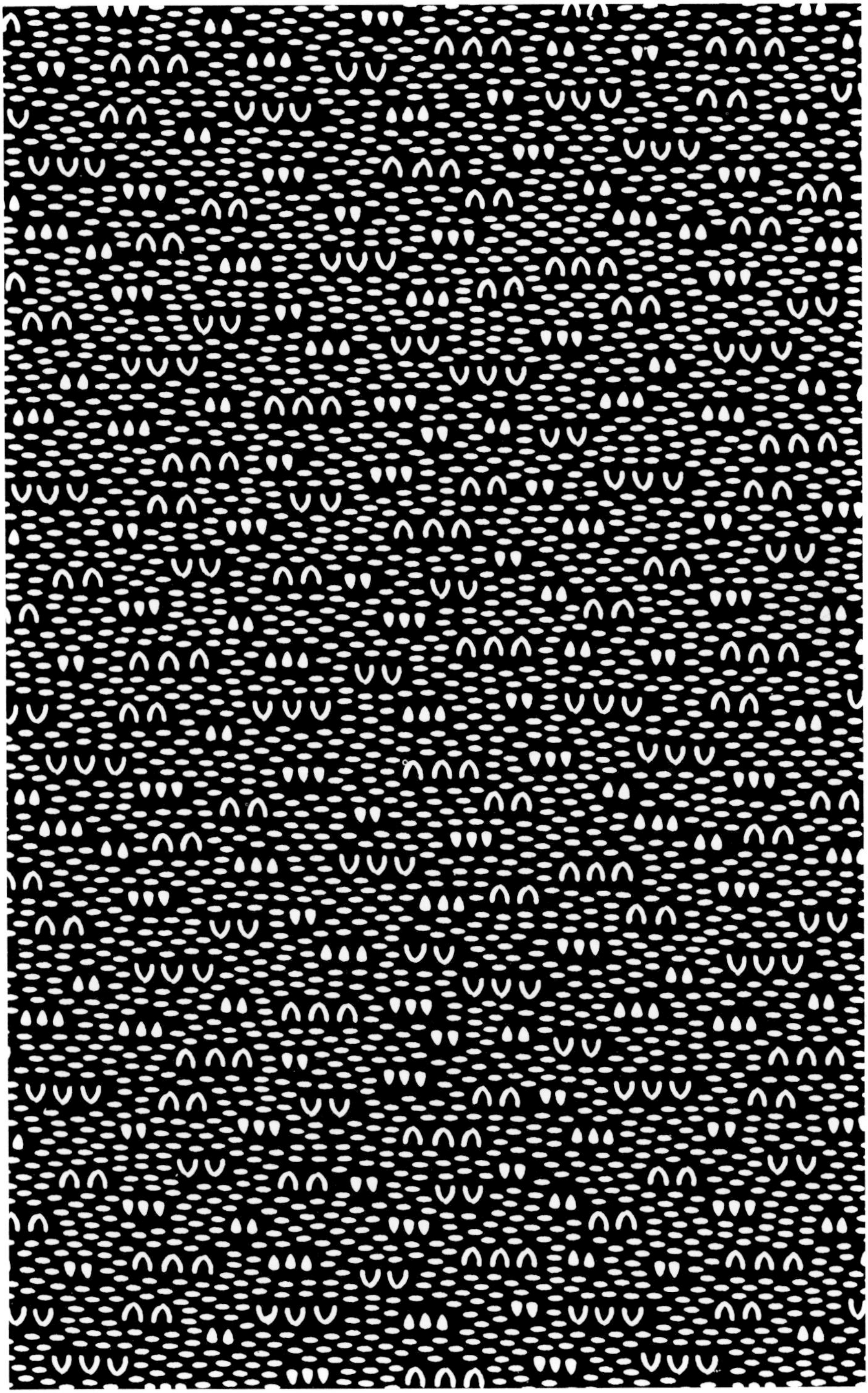

18

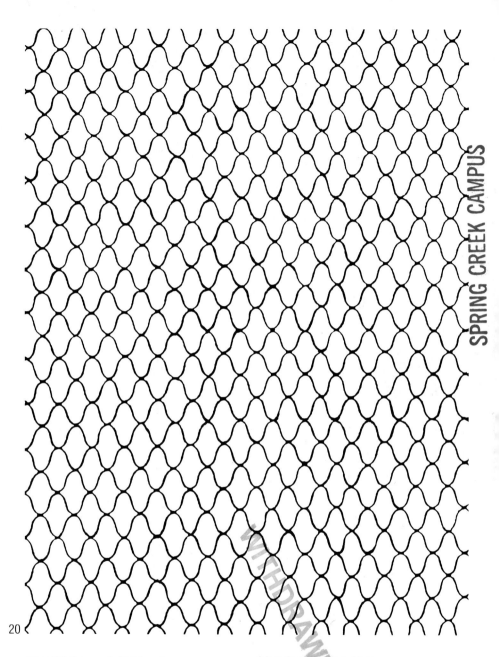

20

19 ■ Wickerwork Plaid

Although the popular image of Edo design is closely linked with the bright, bold patterns of the Kabuki theater, design themes stressing nature and subtlety were also important. This design was loved for its quality of *shibui* (subtle sophistication).

20 ■ *Amime* (Fish Net)

Cool and clean, this simple design inspired by fish net is traditionally printed in blue and white and used for summer kimono and *yukata*. In Edo times, the images and lore of the fishermen made their way into the popular arts and crafts.

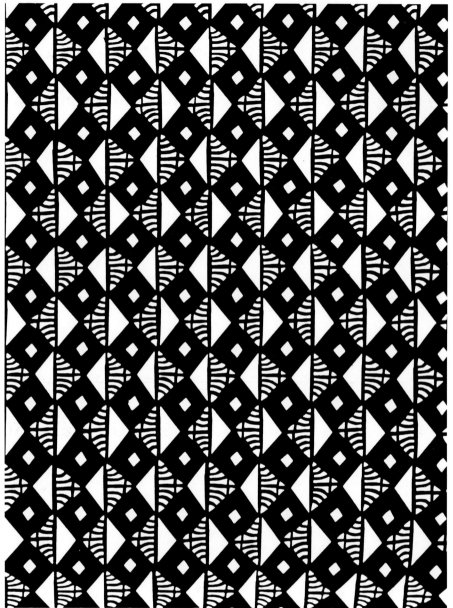

21 ■ Irises and Nail-Pullers
Edo artists rarely employed abstract shapes that had no identifiable referents in their designs. United here are the sublime and the mundane—the iris and the carpenter's tool used to pull nails out of wooden planks. The nail-puller is the diamond flanked by a triangle of irises.

22 ■ Irises and Small Flowers
This seemingly feminine design probably originated in the Kamakura period, when it was used in samurai military dress. In the peaceful Edo period that spanned over 250 years, military patterns like this were adapted for *chiyogami* and used for *origami* and other crafts.

23 ■ Well Frames and Plovers

Only a citizen of Edo would recognize the seemingly incongruous subjects that make up this popular abstract pattern. The crossed wings of the soaring plover break the tranquil space where well frames float languidly across the design.

24 ■ Well Frames in a *Kasuri* Pattern

This sophisticated well frame motif imitates the complex patterns found in *kasuri* weaving, where yarns are dyed in different patterns and then woven together in complicated designs. Traditionally used in children's clothes, such designs are still in everyday use.

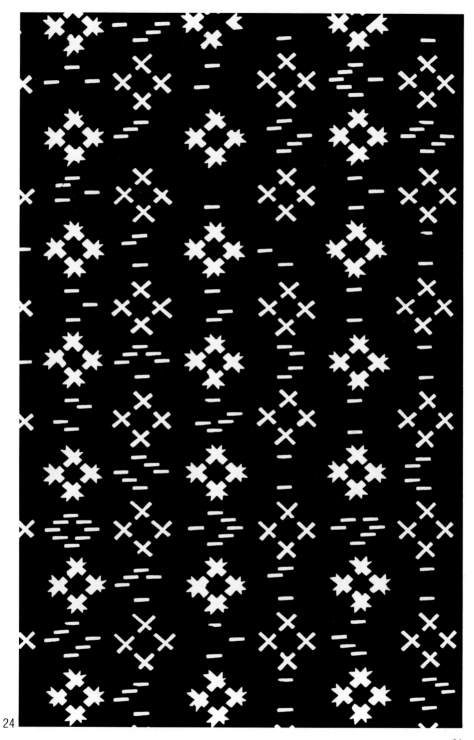

25 ■ *Hanabashi* (Flower Diamond Check)

Small, orderly patterns like this one originated in the Kamakura period and were used exclusively by the samurai to decorate leather armor. Under the Tokugawa shogunate, peace was ruthlessly enforced, and the samurai became anachronistic. Some roamed the country-side as leaderless warriors; others served the shogun in a kind of rough-and-ready police force. Without wars to fight, the samurai eventually lost everything (including their exclusive patterns) to the merchant class.

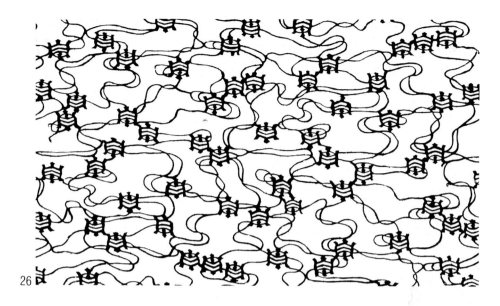

26

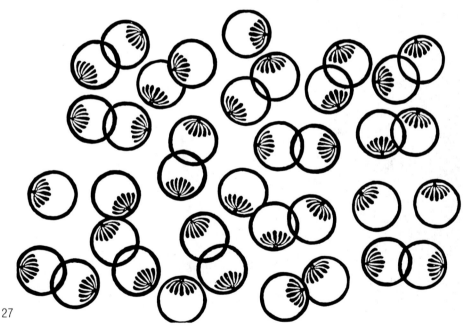

27

26 ■ Bobbins

In this pattern celebrating the tools of the Edo weaver, the artist has created an apparently haphazard design with threads trailing randomly from spool to spool. The balance between image and open space is, in fact, carefully calculated to give the illusion of randomness.

27 ■ *Uchiwa* (Round Fans)

Beyond being useful, the fan was an essential fashion accessory in Edo society. Kyoto's most famous artisan, Miyasaki Yūzen (17th century), was first and foremost a fan painter, whose beautifully painted fans appear in stylish *ukiyo-e* woodblock prints of the period.

28 ■ *Omodaka* (Water Grasses)

The development of precision tools allowed Edo stencil carvers to execute designs with oblique angles and complicated interconnecting patterns. This cool, free-floating design of water grasses calls up images of relaxed summer days in Edo.

29 ■ Baskets and Scattered Apricot Blossoms

A popular kimono choice in Edo times, this pattern of hexagons and apricot blossoms is still worn for wedding parties and special occasions. The floating hexagons use three traditional patterns from the Heian period—scale, *seigaiha*, and basket weave.

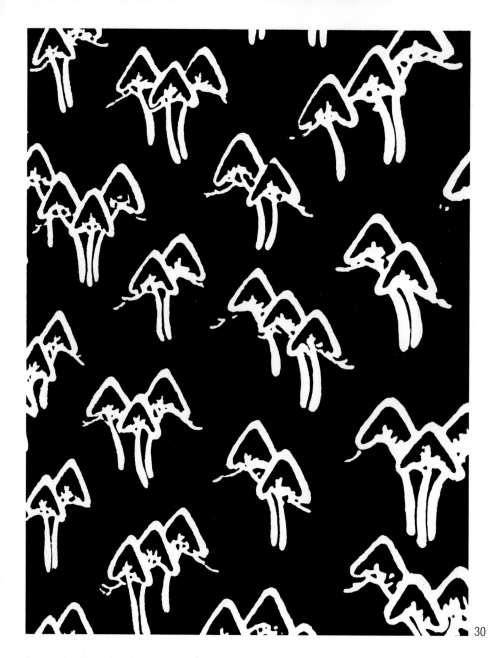

30 ■ *Kasamatsu* (Umbrella Pines)
More reminiscent of the 1950s than the 1650s, this pine tree pattern was often used in *chiyogami*, the brightly colored papers that were so popular in the Edo period. Advanced printing techniques made the previously expensive papers affordable for the average Edoite.

31 ■ Tortoises
At first glance, this pattern appears to be nothing more than a maze—but look again. The "maze" is actually a rather unconventional assembly of tortoises that are randomly connected to one another. This design works well on both cloth and paper.

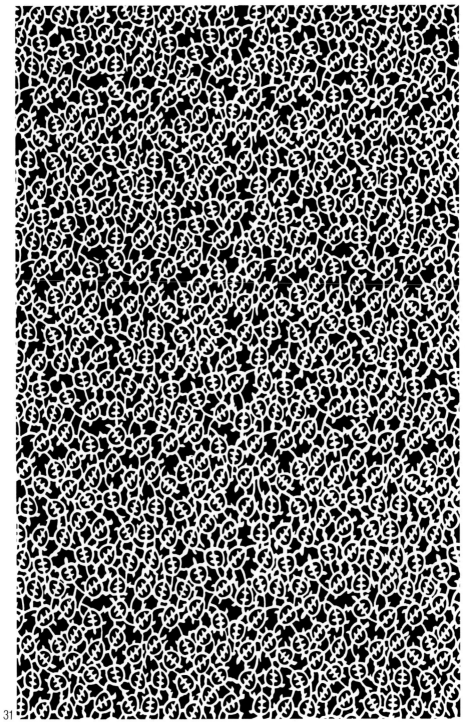

33

32 ■ **Flowered Gates and Rabbits**

On paper, this design showing rabbits coming into and out of flowered gates appears flat and lifeless. In the beautiful kimono of Utamaro's *ukiyo-e* prints, however, the design takes on a different dimension and becomes charmingly sophisticated.

33 ■ **Crows**

This dramatic design is representative of the Edo style made famous by the Rimpa School. Emotional and free in their interpretations of classical themes, these artists often ignored delineations and depended on the sheer energy of brushwork to project their ideas.

34

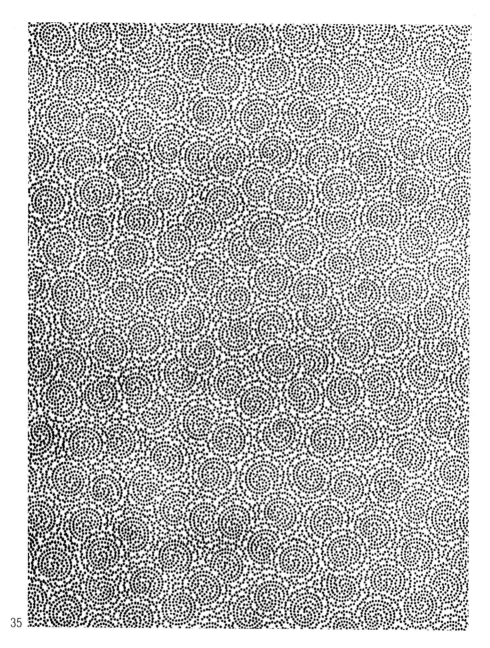

34 ■ Arranged Well Frames

Edo artists typically loved to create new designs by twisting and changing images from classical designs. In this example, the popular well frame motif seems kicked to pieces, and the broken parts are shown from an overhead perspective.

35 ■ Arranged Eddies

The arrangement of dots and open space in this miniature pattern (*komon*) was carefully calculated by the artist to create an image of bubbling, swirling waters. If the eddies had been connected, they would have created a single graphic line and an entirely different look.

36

37

36 ■ Arranged Plaid 1
This is a good example of the bold graphic motifs that became popular in the Edo period. Originating with the brilliantly colored costumes of the Kabuki actors, such designs in more subtle colors were adopted by theater patrons for everyday dress.

37 ■ Arranged Plaid 2
Both delicate and whimsical, this design is a good choice to use in kimono, *haori* (a short jacket), and *chiyogami*. The grid of nine dots, created when the lines of the checkered patterns overlap, adds to the freshness of the plaid.

38

38 ■ Arranged *Manji* (Swastikas)

This pattern is one version of the many designs that originate from the swastika, a Buddhist symbol meaning happiness, benevolence, or an act of charity. Considering the use the Nazis made of this ancient symbol, it is difficult not to react negatively to it now, but the swastika was a mark of good fortune in Edo times. In this pattern, which has a Chinese feeling, the black motifs are organized in a diamond pattern, while the swastikas in the white space resemble *ajiro* (bamboo basket weave).

39 ■ Arranged *Kikkō* (Tortoise Shells)
Still popular in kimono and *haori*, this pattern was borrowed from a traditional brocade (*shokkō*) woven from red, yellow, and indigo threads. The inventive Edo eye arranged the motifs so that the referent is identifiable, but the point of view is strikingly new.

40 ■ Arranged *Miru* (Sea Flowers)
This is one of many ancient patterns that were redesigned by Edo artists in fresh, new ways. In Heian times (794–1185), the *miru* was a floating, circular motif. Here, it is oval and abstracted into a positive-negative play of symbol and space.

41

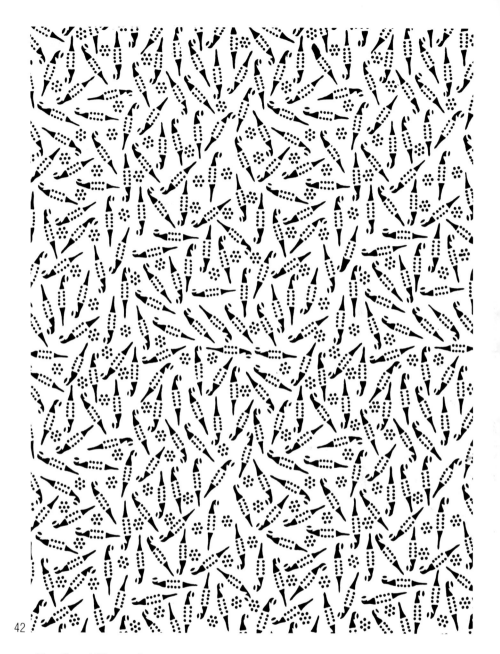

42

41 ■ *Gangi* (Zigzags)

The name of this pattern, which is often used in men's kimono and *yukata*, was inspired by flying formations of wild geese. *Gangi* was considered *iki* (sophisticated) in Edo fashion, where sophistication was at one end of the spectrum and flamboyance at the other.

42 ■ *Kiseru* (Pipes)

In Edo times, these pipes were found in every home in Shitamachi, the shopping, entertainment, and residential districts within Edo (present-day Tokyo). *Kiseru* were smoked by both men and women, a social habit that has long since disappeared.

44

43 ■ *Kikkō* (Tortoise Shells)

The popular *kikkō* pattern originated as a *yūsoku* design that was stenciled onto leather battle gear. The technique disappeared during the 250 years of peace in the Edo period, but the design was retained and reinterpreted as a woodblock print.

44 ■ *Tanabata Matsuri* (Children's Festival) Pattern

This popular children's pattern evokes memories of the *Tanabata* Festival. Each July 7th, Japanese children use paper cutouts and *origami* to decorate bamboo trees, in much the same way Western children decorate Christmas trees in December.

45 ▪ Clouds and Lightning

This dramatic image of lightning (*inazuma*) and swirling clouds (*kumo*) was a restricted pattern for the exclusive use of Fuwa Banzaemon, an actor in the Kabuki play *Sayaate*. The design symbolizes the warrior's legendary strength and fearsome military skill.

46 ▪ Carp Swimming Up a Waterfall

Carp and water grasses weave through the diamond-shaped waterfall to create a rhythmic line pattern. The colors traditionally used in this design—usually blues or bright colors on white—combine to create a cool, summer, watery image.

47

47 ■ *Kōhone* (Water Flowers)

The apparent simplicity of this free-spirited water flower motif is deceptive. The triangle of the water flower leaf and the pentagon shape of the flower have been carefully arranged by the stencil cutter to create a diamond in the open space. Because of the insatiable demand for new kimono designs and the introduction of tools that made such designs possible, the stencil maker became one of the most important characters in Edo's colorful history.

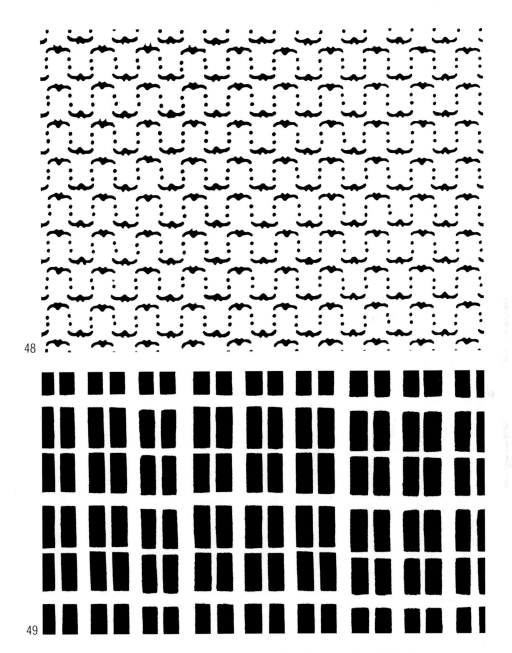

48

49

48 ■ Joined Bats

Popular among the samurai during the Kamakura period, the bat motif was adopted by Edo merchants for use in men's kimono and *yukata*. Note that in this *komon* (miniature pattern), the design is made linear by the dots that join the wings of each bat.

49 ■ Kouraiya-Goushi Plaid

This faux weave (or imitation woven) is composed of thick cross stripes bisected by thin lines, creating a strong and simple geometric print. In subtle colors, the pattern is still popularly used in men's kimono.

50 ■ Scattered Flowers

The strength and longevity of this delight-fully feminine design is in the lightness and precision of the artist's touch. The small flowers were set down in their most elemental forms, and the space was filled with small fragments of the flower motif.

51 ■ Braided Bamboo

This bold basketweave pattern was inspired by *ajiro*, braided bamboo basketry composed of vertical and horizontal lines. The *ajiro* weave was used for many things—from ceiling construction in Edo homes to bamboo fishing nets.

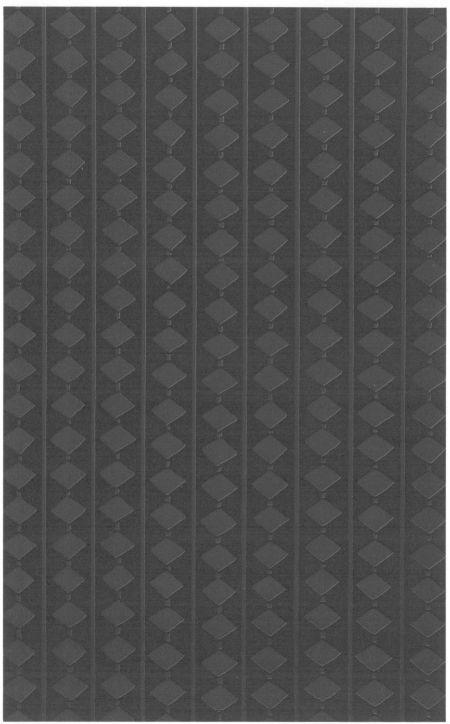

52 ■ Diamond Abacus Stripes

The abacus symbolizes the merchant class, who, though persecuted by the samurai and the nobility, rose to power during the Edo period because of their economic strength. This design decorated the kimono of the tradesmen and survives as a symbol of a new age.

53 ■ *Temari* (Embroidered Balls and Chrysanthemums)

Originating in the Edo period's Kanō School, this festive design is still popular today for women's and children's brightly colored kimono. Patterns such as this are purely Japanese—poetic images free of Chinese influence.

54 ■ Shikan Stripes

This popular Kabuki design appears often in *ukiyo-e* paintings and woodblock prints depicting the Edo theater world. Theatergoing Edoites wore kimono decorated with this pattern in much the same way we wear T-shirts commemorating concerts and sporting events.

55 ■ *Mekago* (Baskets)

Most basketweave patterns, immensely popular in Edo times, were borrowed from basketry used in everyday life. This pattern copies the weave made from wide slices of bamboo used in construction. Edoites loved such clean graphic shapes.

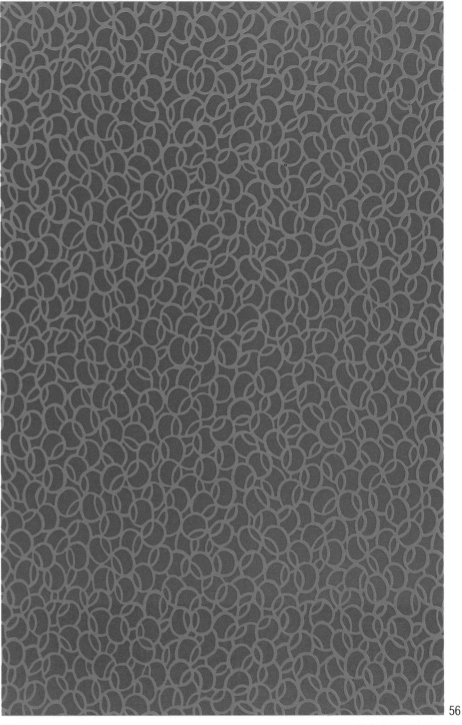

56 ■ *Koko* (Pots)

Koko are bubbling ceramic pots that were found in every Edo household. In this pattern, the pots appear as connecting circles and ovals that tumble exuberantly through the design. The pattern is still printed on brightly colored *chiyogami* and children's clothing.

57 ■ *Kaminari* (Thunderbolts)

Borrowed from Heian times, the square eddy character indicating a thunderbolt symbolizes strength. In Kabuki theater, the warrior hero tied his *kaminari*-decorated kimono with a *shimenawa* (heavy, braided Shinto rope), making a dramatic impression on his audience.

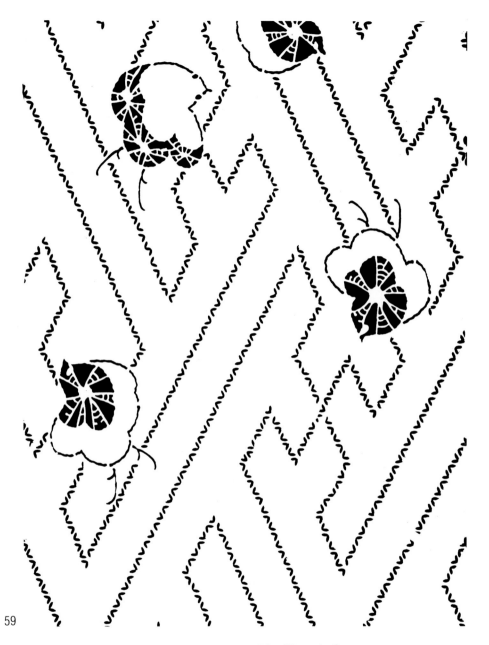

58 ■ *Manji* (Swastikas)
Widely used in Kabuki theater, this
swastika pattern symbolizes strength
when worn by men, a sinister character
when worn by women. The design may
seem flat and mundane on paper; on
fabric, however, *manji* has a depth that
has made the pattern a classic.

59 ■ Plover in *Sayagata*
The plover (a small, short-billed wading
bird) was a popular image in ancient
Japanese arts and decoration. Here, the
plover is decorated with spider webs and
then reduced to its simplest form. Floating in the background are connected
manji (swastikas).

60 ■ Cherry Blossoms and Fans
As the merchants of Edo gained economic power, they began to crave aristocratic trappings, which were technically off-limits. In this pattern, cherry blossoms are combined with the fans used by the nobility, an apparently acceptable compromise.

61 ■ Cherry Blossoms and Mist
This classic Edo pattern was worn in the Kabuki play *Dōjōji* by the character Hanako. The romantic image of weeping cherry blossoms hanging beneath clouds of mist became a much-copied design for fashionable women's kimono.

63

62 ■ *Sai* **(Dice)**

This dice pattern is cleverly composed of side-by-side dice showing only the numbers 3 and 6. These numbers total 9, which was the craftsmen's lucky number and indicated strength. The design was used exclusively to decorate craftsmen's kimono.

63 ■ **Cloisonné**

The origins of this pattern are unknown, but the petal shape may have been inspired by the metal framework used to form a cloisonné design. Brought to Japan from China, cloisonné was a highly prized decoration for boxes, hair ornaments, and other personal objects.

64 ■ Dragons in Clouds

The dragon motif originated with *syokkō*, Chinese brocade brought to Japan in the Heian period. After much reinterpretation, the design became popular in the Genroku era of the Edo period as an *obi* decoration executed in the finest silks and brocades.

65 ■ *Syokkō* and *Chōcho* (Butterflies)

The most highly prized kimono designs of the Edo period were those that contained a riddle or hidden message. In this example of Edo irony, the spider's web held in the wings of the butterfly show that, contrary to expectations, the butterfly has caught the spider.

66 ■ Three Stripes and a Flower

Usually printed on cotton in the cool blues and white favored for summer *yukata*, this design combines three elements associated with the season—*sudare* (a bamboo screen used to shield homes from the intense heat), a languid stream, and scented summer blooms.

67 ■ Stripes and Pine Needle Cranes

It is easy to miss the iconography in this humorous print, though not its joyful effect on the eye. The background stripes are crossed by ribbons of connecting pine needles shaped to suggest soaring cranes, resulting in a sophisticated yet delightful pattern.

68

68 ■ Umbrellas and Misty Cherry Blossoms

On warm spring days, the Edo umbrella maker traditionally took advantage of the sunshine to dry his newly made merchandise. The number of umbrellas in this design suggests that the rainy season was just about to begin. The kind of genre scene depicted here was particularly favored among the many women whose lives were centered on their sumptuous kimono wardrobes.

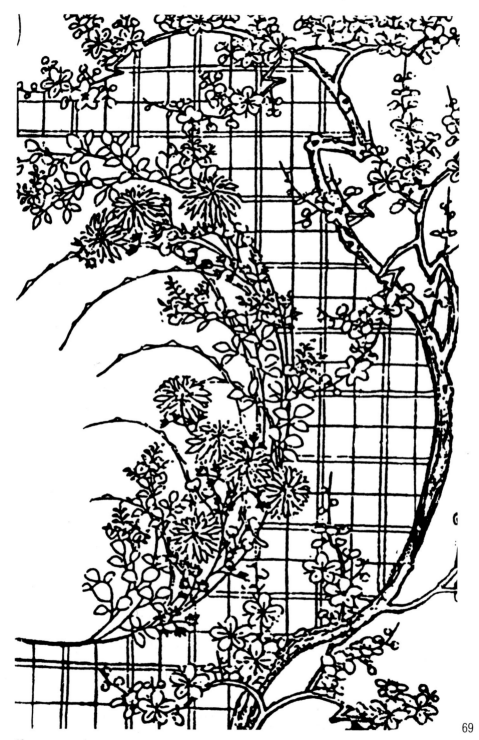

70

69 ■ Apricots and Chrysanthemums in a Drawing Room

This nostalgic pattern recalls the Japan that existed before Westernization. *Ikebana* (a flower composition) sits in a *tokonoma* (alcove), the most honored place in the home. The *tokonoma* sits beside a circular window that lights the scene softly.

70 ■ *Meditai* (New Year's Day Decoration)

This symbolic festival pattern includes the combined images of the *shimenawa* (Shinto rope), the *yuzuriha* (green leaf), and *urajiro* (fir). Together, these images convey the jubilant mood of the New Year's celebration.

71 ■ *Sho*, *Chiku*, and *Bai* (Pine, Bamboo, and Plum)

A famous trio in classic kimono design, *sho*, *chiku*, and *bai* used in combination promised happiness and good luck. Even now, wedding kimono are decorated with pine (for longevity and constancy), bamboo (for rectitude), and plum (for charm and innocence).

72 ■ *Suzume* (Sparrows)

For this type of design, a resist paste was applied through a stencil. The stencils were cut from two sheets of brown paper glued together with a mesh of silk thread between them. Because of their delicacy, the stencils themselves have become collectors' items.

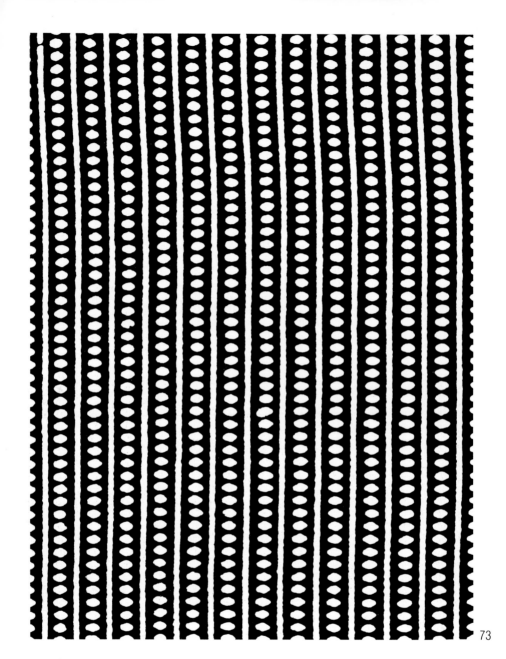

73 ■ *Soroban Jima* (Abacus Stripes)

Before Edo times, stripes were considered commonplace and relegated to the kimono of the servant class. Edo advances in weaving technology, however, created more elaborate and, therefore, more desirable stripe and plaid configurations. Restrictive dress codes under the sumptuary laws also contributed to the popularity of the motif by making it one of the few permitted designs. Businessmen finally took up the stripe, customizing it into printed patterns like the abacus stripe shown here.

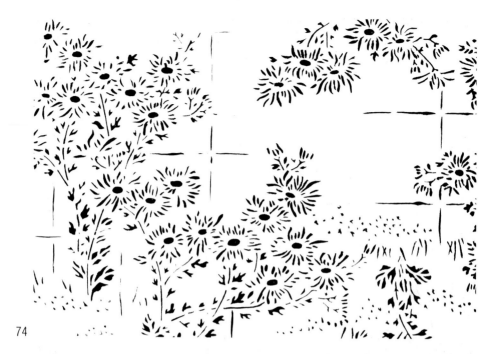

74

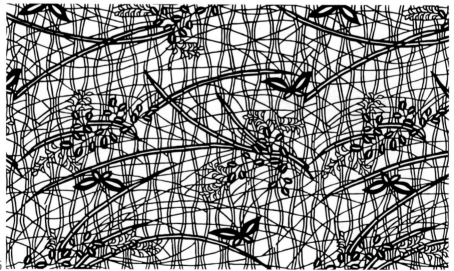

75

74 ■ Chrysanthemums
The chrysanthemum has always been associated with the imperial family and was once forbidden for use by anyone not of royal blood. Many class restrictions were dissolved in the Edo period, however, and images like the chrysanthemum began to be used more freely.

75 ■ Autumn Grasses in *Tatewaku* (Wandering Stripes)
This romantic pattern of autumn grasses and butterflies overlapping on a background of *tatewaku* (wandering stripes) is adapted from *yūsoku* (patterns worn by the court in ancient Japan).

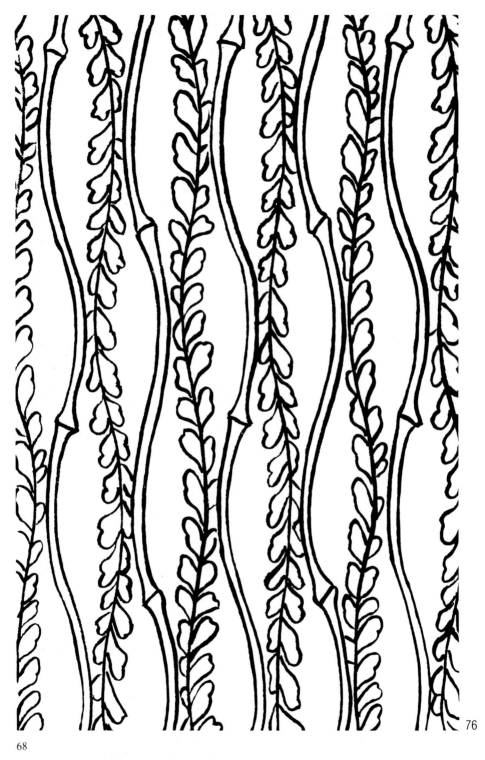

77

76 ■ Bamboo and Wisteria
In the days of strict sumptuary laws that restricted personal extravagance, only the simplest of stripes were allowed in clothing or decoration. As these laws were relaxed, new, imaginative, decorative stripes became the fashion rage of Edo.

77 ■ Cherry Blossoms in Wandering Stripes
Edo artists adapted the wandering stripe pattern and replaced the traditional imperial chrysanthemum with the more common cherry blossom. This pattern, made famous in Kabuki, has a dramatic graphic strength that is intensified by the use of bright contrasting colors.

78

79

78 ■ Bamboo Plaid
This nostalgic diamond stencil design is still used today to decorate kimono and *chiyogami*. The round stencil punch used to execute the design was developed in the Edo period and inspired the many delicate patterns that typify the period.

79 ■ Butterfly Stripes
Straight and curved lines are skillfully combined to create a sequence of abstract butterflies that seem to swing and sway on the page. Grey butterflies on a yellow background would create the illusion that the butterflies are fluttering across a golden field.

80

80 ■ Moon and Ferns

The work of Kyoto's Korin and Yūzen, two of the most important artists of the Edo period, had far-reaching effect on Japanese design of the time. Yūzen, whose name is still a household word in Japan in connection with Kyoto's famous dyeing industry, was actually a fan painter and probably did little dyeing at all. But the designs that adorned his fans were legend and made his work the cutting edge of Edo fashion. This piece is reminiscent of his work.

81

82

81 ■ Ivy, Wheel, and Fan

This design was composed to be independent, perhaps to appear around the hem of a luxuriously colored kimono that had been custom-dyed so that each color was applied individually, image by image. Among collectors today, such kimono are highly prized.

82 ■ Ivy

Originally used in gold on a black lacquer background, this design integrates the ivy vine, leaf, and flower. An open design, it could be repeated in all directions, but is more often seen as an independent image on clothing or lacquer ware.

84

83 ■ Shadow Ivy

The delicate nature of this design—the
fine line background, the soft shadows,
the realistic ivy shapes—could not be
matched today without the use of a laser,
even if the original stencil were available.
This design was probably created as a
special order for a festival kimono.

84 ■ *Tsusumi* (Hand Drums)

This lively, delicate pattern, which was
cut with a round stencil punch, is composed of hand drums set on their sides
and joined together with a curling rope.
Some of the drums appear to have been
set free in space, giving the whole design
a dizzying rhythm.

85

86

85 ■ Cranes, Pine, Bamboo, and Apricot Blossoms

Another version of *sho*, *chiku*, *bai*, this design arranges pine, bamboo, and apricot blossoms to form cranes, the symbol of everlasting fidelity. Such a clever, beautiful design could have been created by Yūzen, who was famous for his visual riddles.

86 ■ Bats and Lanterns

Flying bats were part of the twilight scene in Shitamachi, the main shopping district in Edo. In this punch-stencil design, the lanterns look as if they are ready to be lit. This genre print is typical of the designs used to decorate men's kimono.

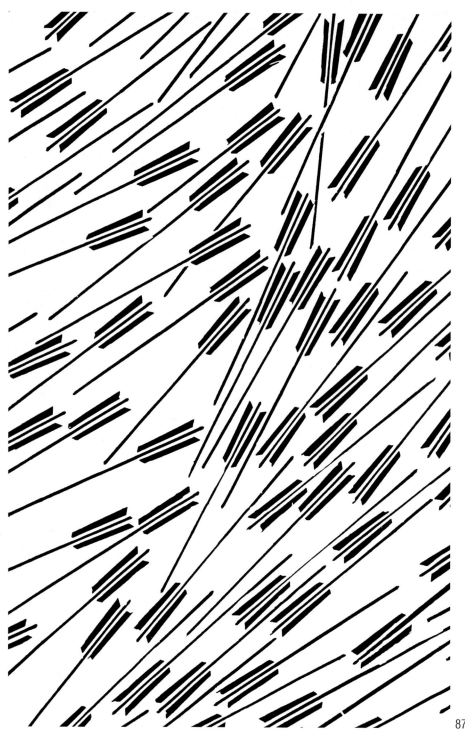

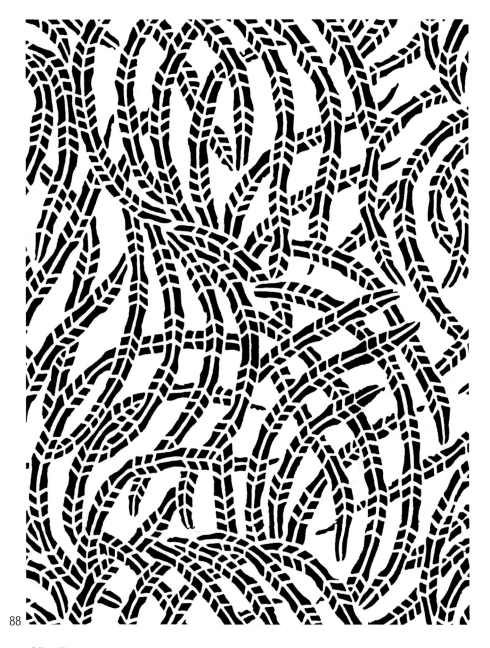

88

87 ■ Flying Arrows

War and the samurai became anachronisms in the Edo period, but the patterns associated with both found a new life with the acquisitive merchant class. This *yagasuri* (arrow) design, originally worn by maids who served the *daimyō* and shoguns, was eventually adopted by Edo townsmen.

88 ■ Plumes

The phoenix, a favorite subject of Japanese artists since the Heian period, has been reinterpreted here by Edo artists in a departure from the norm typical of the times. Only the plumes of the phoenix were used to create a vigorous and original graphic statement.

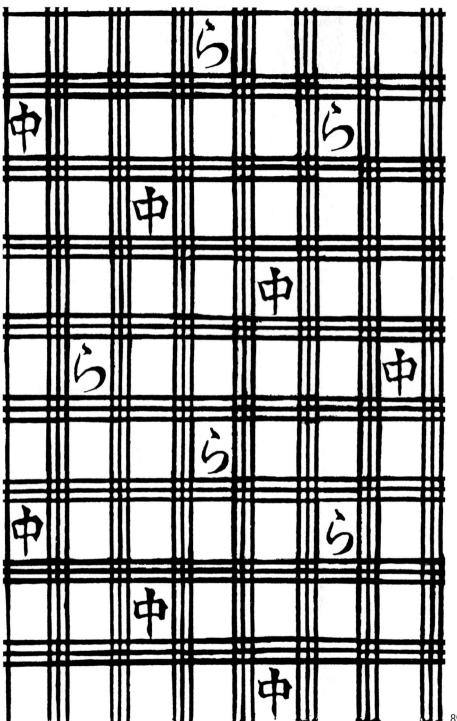

90

89 ■ Nakamura Plaid

This riddle plaid was worn by the Naka-muras, a famous Kabuki family, and their fans. The two Japanese characters, *naka* and *ra*, showed exactly who owned the plaid. Fans wore kimono decorated with the design in much the same way modern baseball fans wear team jackets.

90 ■ Stream and *Momiji* (Maple Leaves)

The maple leaf is one of the most loved images in traditional Japanese design. Here, maple leaves float languidly down a curving stream. This design would be appropriate in a woman's early summer or autumn kimono worn to view the spec-tacular foliage in Kyoto.

91 ■ *Nami* (Waves)

Time and technique merged in the late Edo period to make designs such as this wave pattern a popular choice for both women's and men's kimono. A round stencil punch made ornate, swirling images possible without violating the color restrictions set down in the sumptuary laws. Limited to two colors on cotton —not silk—these punch designs were referred to as "polite waves" or "polite snowflakes"; in other words, they were within the law.

92

93

92 ■ **Waves and Rabbit**

As Westerners see a "man in the moon," Japanese folklore and children's stories talk of a "rabbit in the moon." The images of the rabbit (*usagi*) and the wave (*nami*) are also often combined to decorate children's kites, ceramics, and clothing.

93 ■ **Waves and Dragon**

Always a favorite image of the samurai, who used it to decorate battle armor, the dragon was adopted by Edo Kabuki actors as a symbol of strength and ferocity. In this design, a roaring dragon swims freely among the whirling waves.

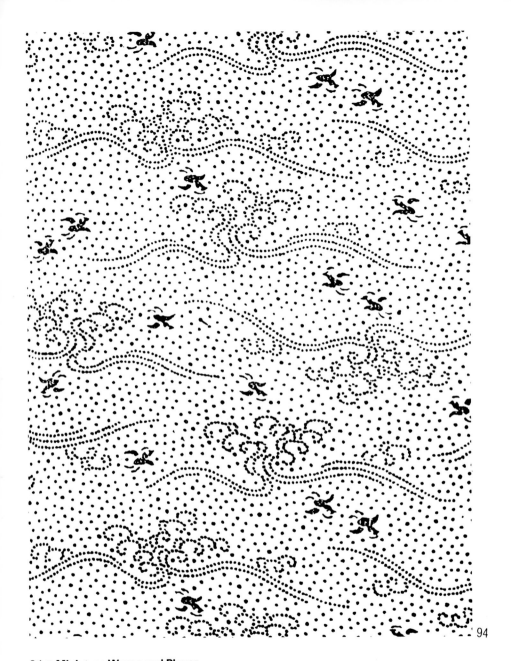

94 ■ Miniature Waves and Plover

The first half of the Edo period was an intensely creative time. After the Genroku era, however, design became a formula, and innovation was sacrificed for ritual and gaudiness. In this stencil punch pattern, the laziness of the late-Edo artists clearly shows. The wave design was already in circulation; the plover was added to make a new image. This change, though not bad, was obviously made for expediency and without the inspiration that characterized early Edo designs.

95

96

95 ■ Well Frames and Patterned Bats
In this design, patchwork *origami* bats fly freely above floating well frames. A good design sense prevails here, because the bat design is ornate, contrasting nicely with the orderly layout of the faux *kasuri* pattern.

96 ■ Streams and Plover
The Edo sumptuary laws prevented citizens from spending their money on such worldly pleasures as silk, bright colors, and elaborate embroidery. Clever designers, however, simply made substitutions (e.g., appliqué for embroidery in this design) with stunning results.

98

97 ■ Batik
Despite trade restrictions, some foreign products slipped into Japan through Nagasaki, where Dutch traders were permitted. Batiks from Java entered the country this way, and this arabesque design imitates the real batik that became the rage of Edo fashion.

98 ■ Chrysanthemum Balls and Arabesque
Heian period *karakusa* (scrolling vine) patterns inspired simplified Edo versions that were used to decorate everyday objects, such as *furoshiki*. This cloth was originally used by bathers at the public baths to wrap their clothes in.

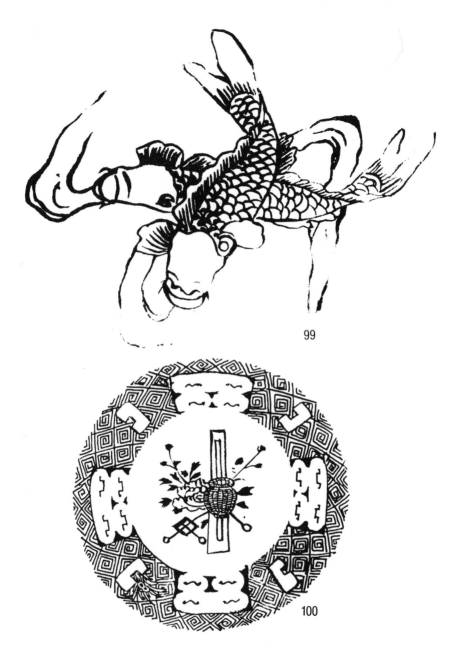

99

100

99 ■ Crossed Carp

When the Tokugawa shogunate banned
Christianity, Christianity went under-
ground. In this crossed carp motif, an
officer of the shogunate might simply
have seen a well-executed design; a
Christian might have recognized the
image of the cross.

100 ■ Key and Handle

The most beautiful and unusual Edo
ceramics came from the kilns of Imari and
Kutani. Inspired by Chinese porcelains
that used a five-color enamel process, an
Imari potter perfected the five-color fir-
ings and then added gold to create the
famous Imari ceramics.

101

101 ■ Chinese Phoenix

This elegant phoenix fills the picture plane with rhythmic, flowing lines. The deep blue and bright white layout and the *mon* (family crest) boldly stamped at the top suggest that this design was used on *noren*, the small curtain indicating that a shop is open for business. Such a pattern could also have been used in Edo times to decorate a fisherman's jacket. Woven of thick, heavy cotton and dyed with indigo, these unique jackets are collectors' items today.

103

102 ■ *Yōrōjima* (Waterfall Stripes)
Yōrōjima is the kind of stripe that would have been considered *iki* (chic) during the Edo period. Partly a reaction to the excesses of the time and partly a compliance with the sumptuary laws, these minimal designs enjoyed tremendous popularity.

103 ■ Congratulations Pattern
Traditionally dyed in blue and white, this dramatic design in Edo times was used as a flag by fishermen to indicate a good catch. Not strictly limited to sea culture, this pattern also appears on *futon* (bedding) of Kanto mountain people.

104

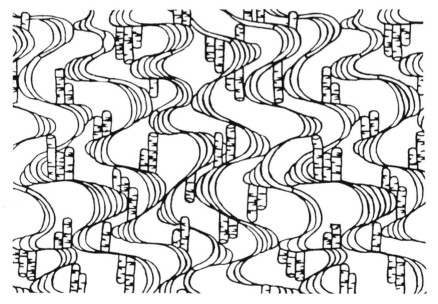

105

104 ■ **Pine Cones and Diamond Bark**
Printed in brown as well as the blue
shown here, this design can still be found
in both kimono and *chiyogami*. The pattern is made interesting by uniting the
seemingly contrary qualities of simplicity
and ornamentality.

105 ■ **Flowing Water and Poles**
This meandering line pattern is still used
for *yukata* that is block-printed in the
traditional summer colors of blue on
white. *Yukata* can be purchased today as
finished garments or, as in Edo times,
custom-made from printed fabric rolls.

106

106 ■ Birds on Waves

The bird-on-waves theme comes from the standard repertory of Heian court designs. This pattern was adapted from a Chinese motif and used to decorate elaborately embroidered kimono and the elegant papers used in scrolls (*karakami*).

In ancient times, such designs belonged exclusively to the aristocracy—a merchant or artisan could never own, let alone wear, such a luxurious pattern. In Edo times, greater numbers of people could enjoy Japan's classic patterns.

108

107 ■ Straw Ropes
This pattern is printed today in white on a deep indigo background. For *ukiyo-e* paintings worn by the beautiful courtesans of the Edo period, however, it was printed on kimono silk in elegant plums and beiges.

108 ■ *Noshi* (Presents)
Japanese use the *noshi* motif as we use wrapping paper and ribbon to decorate a gift suitably for presentation. *Noshi* also has auspicious connotations, making it a good design for the *chiyogami* used to wrap a gift.

109 ■ Floating *Noshi*

This thick- and thin-line composition was executed by a skilled stencil artist. The energy, playfulness, and graphic clarity of the design cause it to pop off the page. The pattern's personality is incredibly contemporary for such an ancient design.

110 ■ Bushclover and *Kikyō* (Balloon Flowers)

The leaves and flowers in this pattern are executed in strikingly different styles. In an example of "image up," simpler flowers fade to the back, and the remaining flowers move out, creating the illusion of perspective and depth.

111 ■ Barley Harvest

Many Edo patterns were made specifically for kimono and laid out according to the way they would fall on the material. In this way, the barley motif is upright around the kimono hem, is horizontal on the side seam, and cascades down the left shoulder.

112 ■ Plectra and Bridges

A pattern for traditional music lovers, this design is composed of parts of the once-common *shamisen*, a stringed instrument whose unique sound was the popular accompaniment for Kabuki plays in Edo times. Today, playing the *shamisen* is considered one of the traditional arts.

113 ■ Flower Baskets

Printed basketweaves were immensely popular during the Edo period and were often styled realistically to resemble bamboo or reeds. In this fantasy design, however, the artist has carefully arranged flower petals to suggest a woven pattern.

114 ■ Scattered Petals

Many scatter prints originated in the restrictive years of the Edo period when the sumptuary laws were in force. Limitations placed on the populace by the shoguns permitted only the simplest and smallest prints, like this one, to be worn on kimono.

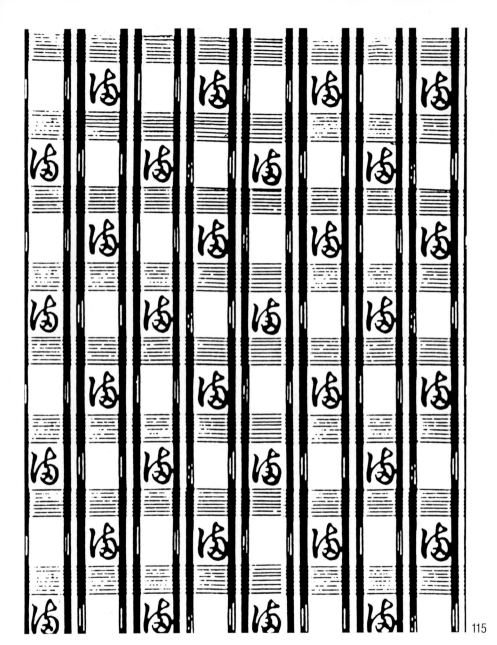

115 ■ Harimaya Plaid

This riddle pattern created for the Harimayas, another famous Edo Kabuki family, identifies the family name: *Hari* (beams), *ma* (the complex character in the center of the plaid), and *ya* (eight) to indicate the eight horizontal lines. The design is graphically strong, emphasizing the force of the family name in the theater world. Worn strictly by family members and followers in Edo times, the design is casually worn today by many people, most of whom have never seen a Kabuki play.

16

117

116 ■ Spring Flowers

The Japanese people enjoy decorations appropriate to the season. This woven basket filled with spring and early summer flowers might appear on a lacquer box or kimono displayed in April, May, and June. After that, the item would be put away until next year.

117 ■ Tidelands and Water Birds

The artist of this design has suggested an entire mood with a few, carefully placed brush strokes. The shapes that compose the soaring birds fit together like pieces of a puzzle; still, each bird has a distinct attitude and personality.

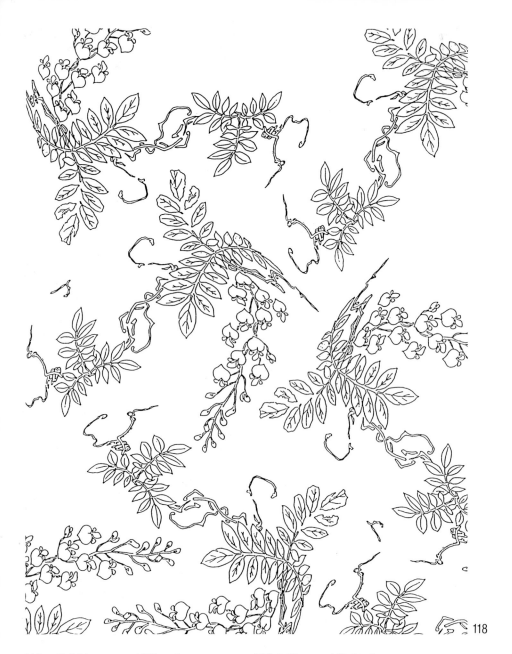

118

118 ■ Gold-Lacquered Wisteria

The image of these flowers and vines appears distorted on the page because the design was originally painted on glass. Sumptuously lacquered and painted with gold leaf, the design was one of the most elegant and sophisticated of the Edo period.

119 ■ Diamond Cutouts

The richness of Edo art and design stems partly from the variety of styles that were freely used during the period. Reminiscent of American Indian patterns, this design has a strong graphic appeal that is strikingly modern.

119

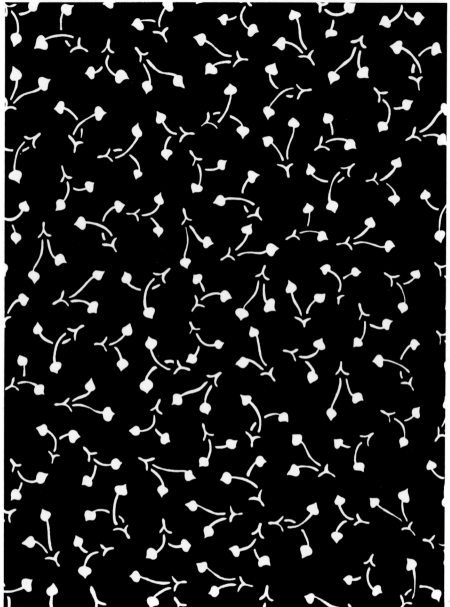

120

120 ■ Hollyhock Leaves

None but the most avid plant lovers pay attention to hollyhock leaves. The Tokugawas, however, adopted them as the family's own *komon* (miniature pattern). This simple scatter version is one of hundreds that adorned the personal property of these famous shoguns.

121 ■ Grapevine and Birds

Originally designed to decorate an Imari sake pot, this pattern was brought to Japan during the Nara period (710–794) via Persia and China. The neat lines and exotic subject matter appealed to Edo artists, who reinterpreted these ancient designs in a contemporary way.

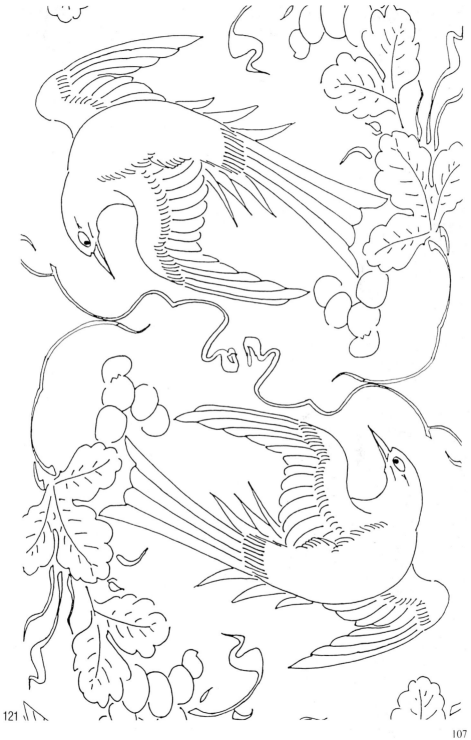

122

123

122 ■ *Hōsyu* **(Jewels) and** *Noshi*

Two lucky symbols are combined here to create this delightful punch design, which is most often used to decorate *chiyogami*. *Chiyogami*, in turn, is used to wrap special gifts. The artist used varying sizes of the stencil punch to create textural emphasis.

123 ■ **Peonies**

Loved for its lavish and gaudy image, the peony was a favorite flower of the Edo period. This design, in which the peonies are outlined with dots, was made using *inden*, a punch technique first used on leather and later used to create texture for kimono design.

124

124 ■ Peony Arabesque

A *karakusa* (scrolling vine) pattern, this version of the peony motif has origins in ancient China. The Edo artist has retained the loose rhythmic styling that is characteristic of the original design, but the execution of the flowers and vines is purely Edo. Simple and clean, this design would be as striking in two colors as one. The popularity of this peony arabesque is affirmed by the frequency with which it appears in woodblock prints of the period.

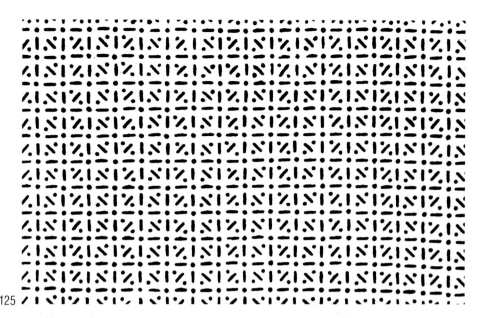

125

126

125 ■ *Masu* (Measuring Boxes)

This visual riddle is definitely intended for use on men's kimono. The broken measuring box in this design contains the Japanese character *sho*, meaning "getting loose." The riddle suggests that the sake or water contained in a broken box will be lost.

126 ■ Pine Bark Diamonds and Chrysanthemums

The chrysanthemums in this complicated pattern have been positioned in front of a kind of curtain. This design is known as *kikumi*, or chrysanthemum-viewing (*kiku* means "chrysanthemum," *mi* means "viewing"), a favorite Japanese pastime in autumn.

128

127 ■ **Water and Rain Dragons**

The dragons in this whimsical stripe pattern seem more like playful pets than the ferocious, fire-breathing beasts ordinarily seen in Japanese design. Perfect for summer *yukata* or children's clothes, this pattern shows the artist's obvious delight in his work.

128 ■ **Water and Balloon Flowers**

Although balloon flowers do not grow in water, the artist unfortunately has taken the liberty of placing them in a stream. Because of the unsettling combination, this pattern has never been popular. Edo artists were very inventive, but sometimes went too far.

130

129 ■ Three Wide Stripes
This dramatic stripe can sometimes be spotted in the *ukiyo-e* prints showing the popular Kabuki actors of the day. Such prints were the *Women's Wear Daily* of their time—printed en masse and used to spread the fashion news from Edo to all corners of Japan.

130 ■ Three-Leaf Hollyhock
Initially stenciled on the Tokugawas' leather gear, this tidy pattern is a nostalgic reminder of the Edo period and the powerful family that controlled Japan for over 250 years. Subtle variations of this motif can be found in diamond, hexagon, border, and stripe designs.

131 ■ _Mujinagiku_ (Chrysanthemum-Filled) Pattern

Chrysanthemum flowers are cleverly composed in this bright autumn image to overlap one another without requiring open space. Distinctly modern in its feeling, this pattern has enjoyed enduring popularity and is still a favorite kimono design.

132 ■ Patterned Bats and Gourds

An ancient Chinese symbol of good luck, the bat motif was embraced by the samurai, picked up by Edo Kabuki actors, and eventually adopted by the merchants of the period. In this design, the bat image is coupled with another lucky symbol, the gourd.

133 ■ Willow Stripes

Next to the cherry blossom, the willow is the most loved of all the Japanese motifs. This simple and elegant stripe was highly regarded in Edo times and is still worn in early summer kimono and *yukata*. Simple though the design may look, its execution —cutting the stencil shapes and keeping them straight—must have been a time-consuming challenge. The resulting design must have been expensive, a fact that would not have gone unnoticed by the money-conscious Edoites.

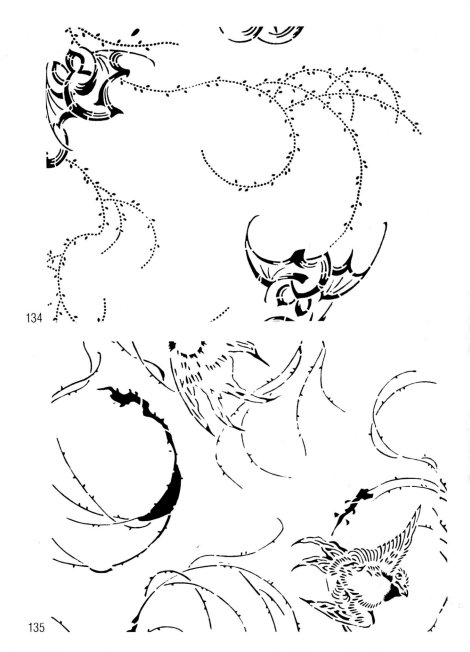

134 ■ Willows and Bats
Both willows and bats in this pattern
appear to flow directly into example 135
below, with the lower bat about to careen
into the soaring swallow. This pattern was
very popular among Edoites, who loved
the curves and smooth elegance of the
design's lines.

135 ■ Early Summer Swallows
Edoites flocked to the countryside in May
to enjoy the new greenery and colorful
blooms. The most loved of all the May
foliage, however, were the yellow-green
leaves of the willow. In this design for
early summer kimono, the swallows add a
graceful, circular rhythm.

136 ■ Willows and Swallows
Finding the swallows in this design is difficult at first because all the lines have the same thickness. There is an energy, here, however, that suggests that the willow has just broken into leaf and the swallow has just arrived to enjoy the pleasures of early summer.

137 ■ Snowflakes and Cherry Blossoms
Snowflakes, which are remarkably large in Japan, were a predominant theme in both *ukiyo-e* woodblock prints and kimono. The snowflakes and cherry blossoms shown here create a bittersweet vision coupling winter's chill with spring's promise.

138 ■ Flowing Water and Cherry Blossoms

In Edo times, the marital status of a young woman could easily be determined by the design and color of her kimono. Unmarried women wore kimono boldly decorated with patterns like this one, often embroidered and colored in bright pinks and reds.

139 ■ Rokuyata Plaid

Rokuyata was a Kabuki character made famous on the Edo stage by the great actor Danjuro. The plaid, which joins three *masu* (measuring boxes), was colored black and white for dramatic effect and was quickly picked up by male patrons of the theater.

140

140 ■ Orderly Pattern

The Edo sumptuary laws not only banned silk and embellishment, but usually restricted the number of colors used in prints to two or three. Plaids and geometrics like this one were popular because maximum effect could be achieved by overlapping colors.

141 ■ Cherry Blossoms on an Orderly Background

The simply drawn cherry blossoms that float across this design become interesting because of the complex woven background they are set against. It was the talent of Edo artists to understand the visual power of combining unlikely objects.

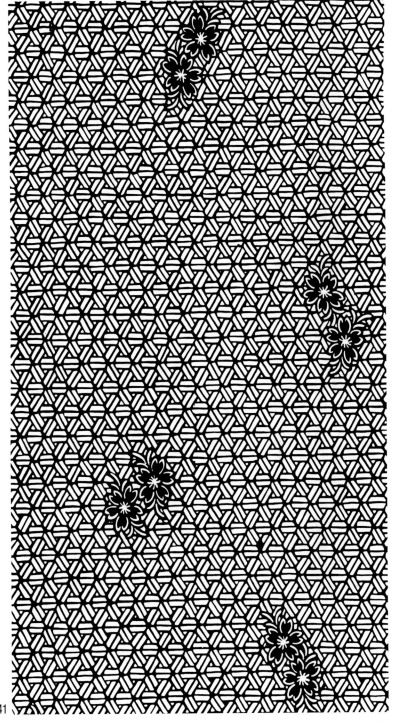

Descriptions of Color Plates

1 ■ Waves and Plover
The two motifs that decorate this gold and lacquer tea box were one of the most popular combinations used in the Edo period. The same images often appeared on *noren*, the small doorway curtains indicating that a shop was open for business.

2 ■ Flowering Plants and Bird
Some of the most ornate and beautiful designs from the Edo period were made for lacquer ware. Favorite themes included exotic birds (like the phoenix) and flowering plants. Many motifs were borrowed from other cultures and then reinterpreted to become distinctly Japanese.

3 ■ Moon and Waves
Typical of the imaginative work produced by Rimpa School artists, this dramatic design for an ocher tea cup was painted by Ninsei Nonomura. Indigo pigment was used for the moon, ultramarine and copper rust for the wave.

4 ■ Magnolia
The pride of Kaga province and the powerful Maeda family, Kutani ceramics are among the most prized in Japan. This spectacular design of magnolia blossoms on a gold leaf background was hand-painted and fired in special kilns.

5 ■ Boat
Simply drawn on lacquer by a skilled hand, this scene shows three men wearing straw hats and rain capes pulling a boat from both sides of a river. Edo artists were the first to decorate valuable lacquer, brocade, and silk with such commonplace images.

6 ■ Snowflakes and Narcissus
The most famous brocades of the period came from the Nishijin in Kyoto, where *obi*, *Noh* costumes, scroll mounts, and treasure covers were intricately woven in the traditional manner. This design combines the finest Edo technical and design skills.

7 ■ Scattered Flowers on Musical Staff
Cleverly resembling a musical score, this design shows whole, half, and quarter cherry blossoms scattered across a staff. The poetic whimsy of the design suggests that the petals could be played as notes in a sweet, languid melody.

8 ■ Arabesque
Vermillion ceramics decorated with a gold leaf technique known as *kinran-de* were among Edo's most highly prized treasures. This design, though originally borrowed from China, has been a part of Japanese art history since Heian times.

9 ■ Paths Through a Rice Field
This aerial view shows a mountain rice field after harvest, with shocks of grass growing along the paths. This design is an excellent sequential pattern that could be continued indefinitely.

10 ■ Turf in the Snow
In this simple yet beautiful design, snow is drawn as a circle and turf as an arc. The images overlap rhythmically in an interplay of darks and lights. The design is still loved for its timeless beauty and is often woven into brocades for *obi*.

11 ■ Cherry Blossoms in the Faraway Mountains
The famous artist Ninsei Nonomura first drew this imaginary spring landscape to decorate a pot. Instantly popular, this poetic vision was reinterpreted and printed on *chiyogami*—inexpensive papers that could be owned and enoyed by everyone.

12 ■ Love Letters
Originally designed for *chiyogami*, these small folded and tied pieces of paper

were used for Edo love letters. The floating white shapes tinged with red and blue
on a dark brown background create an
image as appealing today as in Edo times.

13 ■ Japanese Apricot Blossoms

This design showing brilliant apricot blossoms against a clear blue sky appears to
have been drawn by a child. The spacing
and positioning of the screens, however,
show the artist's great skill in making the
work look deceptively simple.

14–15 ■ *Ebōsho* (Decorated Papers from Kyoto)

More elaborate than the decorated
papers from Edo *(chiyogami)*, *ebōsho*
were often screen-printed and lavishly
decorated, sometimes incorporating
gold into the designs. Often collected
for their beauty alone, these papers were
also used to decorate personal items,
such as tea cases, flower holders, and
umbrella covers.

■ GLOSSARY

Asuka period Japanese historical era (552–710) tremendously influenced by the *Wei* and *Ch'i* cultures from China. Buddhism was introduced to Japan in 530; Prince Shotuku (592–622) established laws that followed Buddhist thought and principles. The Hōryūji Temple in Nara was constructed in the Asuka period.

Chiyogami Rectangular papers decorated with printed patterns and considered to be auspicious. Originating in Kyoto, *chiyogami* became an Edo (pre-Tokyo) phenomenon that paralleled the popularity of *ukiyo-e*. Also used for doll-making and coverings for personal objects, *chiyogami* remains popular today.

Daimyō Provincial feudal lords.

Ebōsho The decorated papers in Edo (Tokyo) that were known as *chiyogami* were called *ebōsho* in Kyoto, which was the earlier capital. *Ebōsho* patterns have a richer character than their bright *chiyogami* counterparts because of their muted colors, stenciling, and sophisticated motif combinations.

Edo period Long, stable, and peaceful Japanese historical era (1603–1868). In 1590, military ruler Tokugawa Ieyasu centered his *bakafu* (tent headquarters) in the remote provincial center of Edo (present-day Tokyo). Eventually, the economic and cultural center of the country shifted from Kyoto/Osaka to the Tokyo plain. The Edo period, which was free of influence from abroad because all foreigners were banned, was noted for its openness and creativity in society and the arts. Popular literature and art flourished in this time.

Furoshiki Literally, a cotton wrapping cloth. Originally used by bathers at the public bath house to stand on while they undressed and then to bundle their clothes in while they bathed. *Furoshiki* was later used as a convenient carryall for everyday items. After the introduction of the shopping bag in Japan, the *furoshiki* began to be used in a ceremonial way as a *noshi*. Wedding gifts, for example,

arrive at the home of the married couples' parents in beautifully dyed silk *furoshiki*.

Heian period Japanese historical era (794–1185) noted for its extraordinary concern for beauty, delicacy, and sensitivity in life and the arts. In 794, the imperial court moved from Nara to Heian Kyo (the capital of peace and tranquility), which was renamed Kyoto eleven centuries later. Under the strong emperors Kammu and Saga during the early part of the Heian period (794–897), Japan maintained active relations with T'ang China. Then, as the power of the emperors began to wane, one family of courtiers—the Fujiwaras—came to dominate affairs of state. After 894, communications with China were suspended, and the period from 897–1185 was called the late Heian, or Fujiwara, period. Japan then sought to develop its own artistic spirit. This shift of emphasis is clearly evident in the evolution of textile design and other arts.

Ikat A variety of predyed cotton cloth with patterns predetermined by the spacing sequences given the weft threads before weaving. The warp (lengthwise) threads are also dyed, and the expertise of the weaver brings the warp and weft threads together perfectly to create a two-dimensional design. In Japan the ikat technique is called kasuri and features various shades of indigo and white.

Ikebana The art of flower arranging. One of the skills that Japanese women must learn to prepare themselves for marriage. There are many methods of *ikebana*, and many schools in Japan teach the different methods.

Iki Literally, chic. Referring to an Edo period stylishness based on savvy, not money.

Imari ceramics Porcelains using a five-color process and gold, named after the port town they were shipped from. In the mid-seventeenth century, brilliantly colored ceramics began to slip into Japan from China. Captivated by the five-colored enameling, a potter named

Higawashima Tokuzaemon from the kiln town of Arita on the southern island of Kyushu worked with other Arita potters to master the process and combine it with gold. Also known as Kakiemon because the glazes had the brilliance and luster of fine brocades, these ceramics are still recognized throughout the world for their exquisite beauty.

Kabuki Japanese theater using dance, music, and mime in elaborately produced historical plays of moral conflict. Makeup and costumes are used symbolically to identify specific character traits. Considered the theater of the common people, Kabuki has been a popular art in Japan since the sixteenth century.

Kamakura period Japanese historical era (1185–1338) noted for its militaristic character. The artistically brilliant Heian period ended in 1185, when, after years of conflict, the Minamoto family defeated the rival Taira family, and military families began their rise to power. Although the imperial court remained in Kyoto, its influence was lessened, and Kamakura in eastern Japan was chosen as the seat of the shogunate. In the arts, the intricate and delicate Heian patterns gave way to the more practical camouflage patterns used to cover armor.

Kanō School See "Tanyu, Kanō."

Karakami Elegant decorated paper originally imported from China to Japan during the Heian period. Also known as Chinese paper, it was made by covering select *torinoko* paper with *gofun* (lime) and printing the design in mica. Highly prized in ancient Japanese society, *karakami* provided the inspiration for the development of Japan's own cultural traditions.

Karakusa Literally, scrolling vine. A sequential pattern that is systematically organized so it can be endlessly expanded. An arabesque motif particularly characteristic of Heian patterns, *karakusa* can be traced from Persia to India, China, Korea, and finally Japan.

Kasuri See "*Ikat*."

Komon Miniature patterns carved into stencils and used in color dyeing. The patterns can be quite large, for some reason, and still be called *komon*. Artisans worked long and hard to design sharp, specialized blades to cut the intricate designs from paper layers strengthened with persimmon juice.

Kusube A dyeing technique used in the decoration of leather battle gear and leatherwear. The discovery of this technique allowed artisans to decorate leather armor with small, fine designs that became closely associated with the samurai class.

Kutani ceramics Porcelains created in the kiln town of Kutani in Kaga province and inspired by Imari ceramics. The Maeda family, patrons of all the traditional arts, sent a samurai to Arita to discover the secrets of Imari. Seven years later, in 1664, the first ceramics noted for their liberal use of brilliant color and sublime decoration were produced in Kutani kilns. The first Kutani master was Morikage, a pupil of Kanō Tanyu. Today, no price is too high for a piece of Kutani bearing Morikage's signature.

Meiji period Japanese historical era (1868–1912) in which Japan fully ended two centuries of self-isolation and welcomed contact with the West and its technological knowledge. By 1868, Emperor Meiji moved with his court from Kyoto to Tokyo, and a constitutional monarchy was formed. With the restoration of the monarchy, the country set out to master the science and technology that made Western nations more economically strong. With the advent of this period, originality ended as Japan began to copy all things Western—dress, furniture, crafts, and art.

Momoyama period Japanese historical era (1576–1603) named after a castle built by unifying *daimyō* Toyotomi Hideyoshi. Hideyoshi stopped the building of temples and started the building of castles in Japan.

Nara period   Japanese historical era (710–794) in which Japan was united for the first time. The period was named after the city of Nara, which is considered the ancient-ancient capital of Japan (Kyoto is the ancient capital). During this period, the Japanese were deeply influenced socially and artistically by Buddhism and T'ang dynasty China.

Noh   Originally theater produced for the enjoyment of the aristocratic and samurai classes. The all-male cast acts, sings, and dances in this first significant Japanese dramatic form.

Nonomura, Ninsei   Most famous potter in seventeenth-century Kyoto.

Noren   A short doorway curtain made of cloth used to signify that shops are open for business. Decorated either with a motif or with the shop's logo, these curtains are also used in homes for eye-level privacy.

Noshi   Literally, a present. This term appears in *hiragana* syllabary as a decorative graphic or as a pattern of tied wrapping bands. Used on a gift to announce respectfully the presentation of the gift. In ancient times, the *noshi* was actually a strip of dried abalone, which was given as a gift on felicitous occasions. In present-day Japan, real dried abalone is only seen on the most expensive gifts. The custom, however, continues graphically—a printed image of the paper-wrapped strip of dried fish is attached to the gift.

Obi   A sash or cummerbund worn with a kimono. There are as many kinds of *obi* as there are fabrics, colors, and designs. The correct *obi* choice depends on the kimono, the season, the occasion, and whether the wearer is married or single. Often handwoven, the *obi* itself is a work of art.

Origami   Literally, folded paper. This art form has its origins in the rituals of Shinto and Buddhist services, in which this folded paper was used to represent life forms. In addition to fulfilling a religious purpose, *origami* was an amusement and became increasingly popular as such among young and old alike. *Origami* is usually made from a paper rectangle or square colored and patterned to reflect the character of the object fashioned.

Rimpa School   Term associated with artists in the sixteenth and seventeenth centuries who specialized in the reinterpretation of ancient subjects in a fresh, sometimes startling new way. Beginning with Hon'ami Kōetsu (1558–1637) and the artists who surround him, the Rimpa School artists produced art, craft, and calligraphy of unparalleled quality and diversity that was inspired by the classical subjects of the Heian period. The Rimpa artists produced work of a standard that had not been seen in Japan since ancient times.

Tanabata matsuri   A festival held throughout Japan on July 7th each year celebrating the celestial meeting of the Princess Weaver Star and the Herdsman. Symbol of the festival is the *tai* (snapper fish), and large floats in the shape of this fish are dragged through the streets by the young men of the town. Children take part in the festivities by pulling smaller carts of the same design, with the tail of the *tai* wiggling realistically behind.

Tanyu, Kanō   Grandson of the famous Eitoku, who painted the golden screens for Hideyoshi, Kanō Tanyu perpetuated the reputation of his family's august tradition in the early part of the seventeenth century. Kanō Tanyu and members of the Kanō School painted for Tokugawa Ieyasu at Edo Castle and Nijo Castle in Kyoto. Attuned to the Ieyasu ideals of frugality and simplicity, this early work, which set the standard for the Edo period and all Japanese refined taste since, acknowledged the Chinese heritage but interpreted traditional themes in a manner that has become recognized as distinctly Japanese.

Uchiwa   Round, flat, unfoldable fans, made of handmade paper (*washi*) and